H2O A JOURNEY OF FAITH

PARTICIPANT'S GUIDE

H2O A JOURNEY OF FAITH

PARTICIPANT'S GUIDE

THOMAS NELSON

Since 1798

NASHVILLE DALLAS MEXICO CITY RIO DE JANEIRO BEIJING

The publishers are grateful to Ross Brodfuehrer for his collaboration and writing skills in developing the content for this book.

Published in association with the literary agency of Yates & Yates, LLP, Attorneys and Counselors, Orange, California.

Published in Nashville, Tennessee, by Thomas Nelson. Thomas Nelson is a registered trademark of Thomas Nelson, Inc.

Thomas Nelson, Inc. titles may be purchased in bulk for educational, business, fund-raising, or sales promotional use. For information, please e-mail SpecialMarkets@ThomasNelson.com.

Unless otherwise noted, Scripture quotations are taken from the HOLY BIBLE: NEW INTERNATIONAL VERSION®. Copyright © 1973, 1978, 1984 by International Bible Society. Used by permission of Zondervan Publishing House. All rights reserved.

Scripture quotations marked CEV are from THE CONTEMPORARY ENGLISH VERSION. © 1991 by the American Bible Society. Used by permission. Scripture quotations marked GNT are from THE GOOD NEWS TRANSLATION. © 1976, 1992 by The American Bible Society. Used by permission. All rights reserved. Scripture quotations marked MSG are from The Message by Eugene H. Peterson. © 1993, 1994, 1995, 1996, 2000. Used by permission of NavPress Publishing Group. All rights reserved. Scripture quotations marked NCV are from the New Century Version®. © 2005 by Thomas Nelson, Inc. Used by permission. All rights reserved. Scripture quotations marked NIRV are from the HOLY BIBLE, NEW INTERNATIONAL READER'S VERSION™. © 1995, 1996, 1998 by International Bible Society. Used by permission of Zondervan Publishing House. All rights reserved. Scripture quotations marked NLT are from the Holy Bible, New Living Translation. © 1996. Used by permission of Tyndale House Publishers inc., Wheaton, Illinois 60189. All rights reserved. Scripture quotations marked NLV are from the New Life Bible, copyright © by Christian Literature International. Used by permission. All rights reserved. Scripture quotations marked PHILLIPS are from J. B. Phillips: THE NEW TESTAMENT IN MODERN ENGLISH, Revised Edition. © J. B. Phillips 1958, 1960, 1972. Used by permission of MacMillan Publishing Co., Inc. Scripture quotations marked TLB are from The Living Bible. © 1971. Used by permission of Tyndale House Publishers, Inc., Wheaton, Illinois 60189. All rights reserved.

MERE CHRISTIANITY by C. S. Lewis copyright © C.S. Lewis Pte. Ltd. 1942, 1943, 1944, 1952. Extract reprinted by permission.

ISBN: 978-1-4185-3392-2

Printed in the United States of America
09 10 11 12 13 RRD 5 4 3 2 1

Contents

Water. Our world couldn't exist without it. It covers our planet and fills our bodies. It keeps us alive. Jesus knew how important water was. Maybe that's why He called Himself the Living Water. He was making a claim and an offer too good to ignore. H2O is about water, the Living Water Jesus said He offered. If you're thirsty, you owe it to yourself to consider what He said . . . and who He is.

We are glad that you are taking part in H2O. We don't think you'll regret it.

The idea of these sessions is to explore Jesus, who He was and is, what He said, and what that means for you. There will be no heavy-handed preaching or manipulation. As a matter of fact, each group will abide by these principles:

Ground Rules

- Everyone is free to express his or her views, whether he or she is in agreement with the DVD message or not.

- No one is allowed to criticize or attack someone else's view, although you may express your own when it disagrees with someone else's.

- No one has to talk at all. You can simply sit and listen, if you prefer.

- Conversely, no one is allowed to talk all the time.

- We will start the dinner at _____ o'clock and end each session by _____ o'clock.

Each gathering will include a meal, a half-hour DVD presentation, and an open discussion. So, what's there to lose? Not much but some time out of your week. What is there to gain? At the very least, a deeper understanding of what others believe and why. At the most, if what Jesus says is true, a way to quench the deepest thirsts of your life.

This participant's guide will be your partner as you watch the ten compelling dramas in the H2O DVD series. The sessions outlined here will help you remember what you see and express how you feel about it. For each week you will see a section for Discussion and a section for Reflection. The Discussion section contains questions intended to guide the discussion for your group meeting. The Reflection section is for you to continue thinking and reflecting on your own throughout the week.

You're ready to get started. We hope you will enjoy this unique journey of discovery and faith.

EPISODE 1

Thirsty

DISCUSSION

1. Kyle defined *thirst* as an inner desire that demands satisfaction and said that people are thirsty for something that can't be satisfied with the stuff of this world.

   § What are your feelings about Kyle's statement?

§ If you feel people do experience that kind of deep thirst, how would you describe it?

§ If you don't think there is such a thirst, then how do you explain so many people feeling as though there is?

2. Oxford scholar C. S. Lewis was quoted in the presentation.

Creatures are not born with desires unless satisfaction for those desires exists. A baby feels hunger: well, there is such a thing as food. A duckling wants to swim: well, there is such a thing as water. . . . If I find in myself a desire which no experience in this world can satisfy, the most probable explanation is that I was made for another world. If none of my earthly pleasures satisfy it, that does not prove that the universe is a fraud. Probably earthly pleasures were never meant to satisfy it, but only to arouse it, to suggest the real thing.

—C. S. LEWIS, *Mere Christianity,* p. 120, MacMillan, NY, 1979

Here are some other desires and their means of fulfillment:

DESIRE	FULFILLMENT
thirst	water
knowledge	information
companionship	people
children	procreation
accomplishment	success
recognition	awards

⚘ Can you think of others to add to the list?

DESIRE	FULFILLMENT

§ Besides the deep-down thirst Kyle was talking about, can you think of a desire for which there is no fulfillment on earth?

3. Kyle suggested five ways we could view the possible fulfillment of our deepest thirst. As you approach this study, how would you describe your attitude? Would you say you are more cynical, skeptical, curious, settled, or satisfied?

- Cynical—certain that pretty much everything is a scam

- Skeptical—suspicious of everything (politicians, preachers, even your own brother!) and need clear proof before trusting anything

- Curious—interested in finding truth and open to whatever it may be

- Settled—fairly content but knowing that your deepest longings are not being met

- Satisfied—certain you have found what you are looking for and, as a result, thoroughly fulfilled

§ Why do you say so?

4. Do you really believe Mandi lost her wedding ring in the ocean and then Vince and Kyle found it later with an underwater metal detector in near total darkness?

- "No way! That has to be bogus."

- "It's doubtful. I'd have to see some convincing proof."

- "It's possible. I'd be interested in hearing more about it."

- "Who cares? What does it matter?"

- "I'm not sure, but I do know I've had equally thrilling experiences in my life."

If you said . . .

- "No way! What a fake," then you are probably a cynic.

- "It's doubtful. I'd have to see more proof," then you are probably a skeptic.

- "That's interesting. I'd like to hear more about it," then you are probably curious.

- "Who cares? What does it matter?" then you are probably someone who settles for what you have and doesn't look for more.

- "I'm not sure it's true, but I've had thrilling things happen in my life," then you are most likely learning to be satisfied.

§ Do you find this assessment to be an accurate gauge of your attitude toward new information in life?

5. What do you think is the likelihood that Jesus can fill a person's deepest thirst? What makes you think so?

REFLECTION

These are optional thought questions to ponder or respond to in writing between sessions. You will *not* be asked to share your answers in the next session, but you may find it helpful to talk them over with a friend.

1. Is there anything you picked up from the DVD or group time that you would like to think more about or be sure to remember?

2. Try to describe your own deep thirst, if you feel you have one.

3. Do you experience this thirst at certain times more than others? If so, when are those times of intensified thirst?

4. Why might you feel this thirst more at these times?

5. What have you found to be the thirst-quenching ability of the items listed below? Circle your answers.

Money	Zero	Low	Medium	High	Complete
Possessions	Zero	Low	Medium	High	Complete
Success	Zero	Low	Medium	High	Complete
Relationships	Zero	Low	Medium	High	Complete

6. When you do get thirsty in the deeper sense, what do you generally turn to in order to quench your thirst? Describe how well it works.

Jesus stood and said in a loud voice, "If anyone is thirsty, let him come to me and drink."
—**JOHN 7:37**

EPISODE 2

Polluted

DISCUSSION

1. Kyle used words like *boring*, *outdated*, and *hypocritical* to describe a lot of people's experience of church. What words would you use to describe your experience of church?

2. If you had to describe Jesus from your church experience alone, what would you say He is like? How close do you think this church view of Jesus is to the real Jesus?

3. When Kyle went door to door asking people why they didn't attend church, he found that most people didn't say things like, "I don't believe in God" or "I think the Bible is a bunch of fairy tales." Instead, he heard things like, "Church is boring" or "I don't understand what the preacher is talking about" or "I'm busy."

§ When it comes to faith, would you say your primary problem is with Jesus and what He is like or with the church and what it is like? It could be with both, but if it is both, with which do you have a bigger struggle—Jesus or the church?

4. One of the perversions of Christianity is turning it into a bunch of rules. When Kyle was talking about this, he listed some old laws that were pretty funny.

§ Which of these laws do you think should still be on the books?

FOR	AGAINST	
		A person may not wear cowboy boots unless he owns at least three cows.
		Owners of homes with Christmas lights up past February 2 will be fined $250.
		Gathering and consuming roadkill shall be illegal.
		No more than five inoperable vehicles may occupy one piece of property at one time.
		A woman may not buy a hat without her husband's permission.
		Women should not be allowed to drive motorized vehicles unless a man precedes them waving a red flag to warn oncoming pedestrians or motorists.

5. There are a lot of dos and do nots in the Bible, and that is why a lot of people think being a Christian is all about following rules. But the Bible says that one reason God gave all these rules was to make it clear that people cannot follow all the rules—that perfect rule-based living is impossible.

Now do you see it? No one can ever be made right in God's sight by doing what the law commands. For the more we know of God's laws, the clearer it becomes that we aren't obeying them.
   —ROMANS 3:20 TLB

So what was the law for? It was given to show that the wrong things people do are against God's will. . . . In other words, the law was our guardian leading us to Christ.
   —GALATIANS 3:19, 24 NCV

§ Would you agree that following all the right rules and doing everything perfectly is impossible? Why or why not?

6. Besides rule-based living, Kyle mentioned other distortions of Jesus' message. He talked about what one writer termed "Christianity and _____"; that is, stuff added to Jesus like political and social agendas, or even personal opinions. He said such additions are like nasty ranchero sauce added to a good burrito.

§ What have you seen added to the basic message of Jesus?

7. In the DVD, the minister reads Luke 15:1–2 from the Bible:

> *Now the tax collectors and "sinners" were all gathering around to hear him. But the Pharisees and the teachers of the law muttered, "This man welcomes sinners and eats with them."*

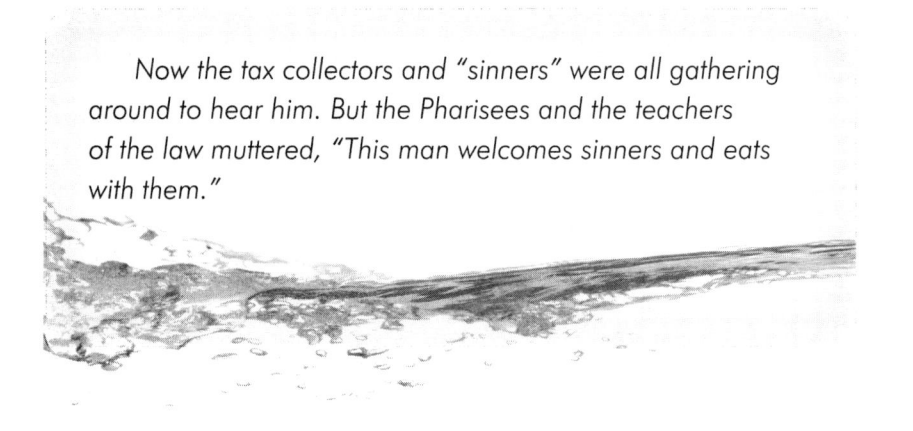

§ The religious leaders of His day saw Jesus as a person who readily connected with those whom others viewed as immoral. How close is this description to your view of Jesus? Would you say pretty close? Or quite distant? Why?

8. Are you willing to consider Jesus on His own terms, apart from how today's church might represent Him?

REFLECTION

1. Of the pollutants Kyle mentioned, which has particularly bothered you?

    ____ the boring, monotonous nature of so many churches

    ____ making following Jesus all about keeping certain rules

    ____ political or social agendas, and personal opinions added onto Jesus' message

    ____ the hypocrisy of those who claim to be following Him

    ____ the general weirdness of Christians

    ____ something else: _____

2. If you had an important message to tell the world, but other people came along and twisted, polluted, and added to it, how would you feel?

3. What would you imagine to be Jesus' reaction to the abuses and misuses of His message?

4. The Bible actually tells us to not blindly trust people, *especially* those who claim to be communicating messages from God. That's because people will let us down. People will intentionally mislead. People are polluted. John, one of Jesus' closest followers, wrote:

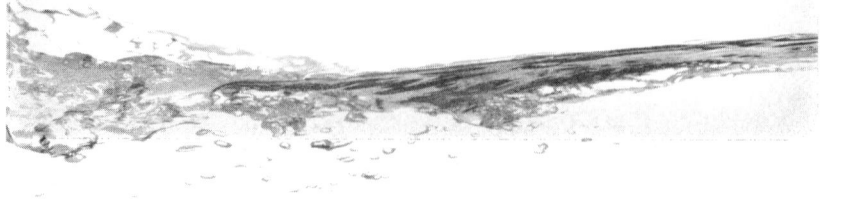

> My dear friends, don't believe everything you hear. Carefully weigh and examine what people tell you. Not everyone who talks about God comes from God. There are a lot of lying preachers loose in the world.
> **—1 JOHN 4:1 MSG**

§ Try writing out your view of Jesus; that is, try to describe Him as you see Him.

5. Where did you get your information for what you just wrote? Check all that apply.

_____ from accounts of Him recorded in the Bible

_____ from what I've read in books or magazines

_____ from how the church represents Him

_____ from the way Christians act

_____ from the attitudes of my parents, professors, friends, etc.

§ Which aspects of your view came from eyewitness descriptions of Him like those found in the Bible? Circle them.

§ Which came from less-than-reliable sources? Cross them out.

§ Which came from . . . well, you don't know where? Put a question mark beside those.

6. The preacher in the DVD described Jesus this way.

- The love of Jesus is not conditional.

- It isn't based on ulterior motives.

- It has no hidden agendas.

- There's nothing you can do to deserve it.

- And there's nothing you can do to lose it.

- It's free. It's powerful. It's pure.

§ Are you willing to consider Jesus on His own terms, to see if He is like what this preacher described?

Never will I leave you; never will I forsake you.
—HEBREWS 13:5

NOTES

DISCUSSION

1. Who did you find yourself identifying with, or resonating with, most: the Korean American girl, her mother, Kyle's daughter, or Kyle as the good dad?

2. What is your reaction to the fact that the most common descriptive name for God in the New Testament is "Father"?

3. Here are some descriptive words for God based on the Bible.

√   Check those you believe are absolutely true of God.

X   Mark an X beside those you believe are NOT true of God.

?   Place a question mark beside those about which you just aren't sure.

___ living (alive)	___ infinite (no beginning or end)	___ eternal
___ omnipotent (all-powerful)	___ omniscient (all-knowing)	___ omnipresent (present everywhere)
___ holy (perfect)	___ wise	___ impartial
___ loving	___ patient	___ compassionate
___ forgiving	___ faithful	___ generous
___ kind	___ responsive	___ personal

Total checkmarks in shaded area: ____

Total in unshaded area: ____

4. One inaccurate view of God is that of an angry father. You may wonder why negative words such as *angry* are not on this list describing God. While anger may be a temporary reaction to evil, a reaction that flows out of God's holiness, anger is not an ongoing characteristic of God as He is in and of Himself. Look at the Scripture below:

His anger lasts only a moment, but his favor lasts a lifetime.
—PSALM 30:5

A good parent might sometimes get angry, but anger is not who he or she is. That's how the Bible describes God: He may get angry, but He is not angry in the same way He is loving or kind.

§ Do you think this distinction between what God sometimes does and what He is in and of Himself is valid? Why or why not?

5. Mark a *D* at the place on each line that depicts how you experienced your dad when you were little, say, in elementary school. If you didn't have a dad, choose the closest person you had to a father figure.

§ Next put a *G* on each line at the place that represents how you see God these days.

Gentle	___	___	___	_G_	___	_D_	___	___	Stern
Close	___	___	___	___	___	___	___	___	Distant
Talkative	___	___	___	___	___	___	___	___	Silent
Patient	___	___	___	___	___	___	___	___	Explosive
Joyful	___	___	___	___	___	___	___	___	Somber
Encouraging	___	___	___	___	___	___	___	___	Critical
Interested	___	___	___	___	___	___	___	___	Apathetic
Kind	___	___	___	___	___	___	___	___	Harsh
Honest	___	___	___	___	___	___	___	___	Deceitful
Consistent	___	___	___	___	___	___	___	___	Erratic

§ How is your experience of your dad when you were a kid similar to how you see God now? What does this exercise show you, if anything?

6. Would you welcome or resist the concept of a loving heavenly Father? Why?

7. What impact would it make on your life if you did see God as a patient, loving, forgiving Father?

REFLECTION

1. During the group discussion, you were asked to mark which of the characteristics of God seem true to you, which seem false, and which you were unsure of. Look at them again, but this time think of them in terms of which ones you *experience* as you relate to God. For instance, you may think that God is kind, but you may not experience this kindness when you try to relate to Him.

E   Place an *E* beside those you experience personally

B   Place a *B* beside those you believe but do *not* experience

___ living (alive)	___ infinite (no beginning or end)	___ eternal
___ omnipotent (all-powerful)	___ omniscient (all-knowing)	___ omnipresent (present everywhere)
___ holy (perfect)	___ wise	___ impartial
___ loving	___ patient	___ compassionate
___ forgiving	___ faithful	___ generous
___ kind	___ responsive	___ personal

What did this exercise reveal to you, if anything?

2. Here are some reasons a person may resist the idea of God being a loving Father. If you find yourself pushing away any thought of a loving heavenly Father, do any of these lie beneath that resistance?

_____ I just don't believe it's possible that God is like that.

_____ I feel so unworthy of that kind of love.

_____ I used to believe it, but too many bad things have happened to me.

_____ I've been burned too many times when I've trusted someone to be loving.

_____ I don't want to believe in a God of any kind, because that would mean I have to do things His way.

_____ I am uncomfortable with the experience or feeling of love. It's just too . . . squishy!

_____ Other: _____

3. You might want to slowly make your way through these Scriptures that highlight God as Father. Underline anything that stands out to you.

A father to the fatherless, a defender of widows, is God in his holy dwelling.
—PSALM 68:5

Which of you, if his son asks for bread, will give him a stone? Or if he asks for a fish, will give him a snake? If you, then, though you are evil, know how to give good gifts to your children, how much more will your Father in heaven give good gifts to those who ask him!

—MATTHEW 7:9–11

One day Jesus was praying in a certain place. When he finished, one of his disciples said to him, "Lord, teach us to pray, just as John taught his disciples." He said to them, "When you pray, say: "'Father, . . .'"

—LUKE 11:1–2

For you did not receive a spirit that makes you a slave again to fear, but you received the Spirit of sonship. And by him we cry, "Abba, Father." The Spirit himself testifies with our spirit that we are God's children.

—ROMANS 8:15–16 (Abba is Aramaic for "Daddy")

Give praise to the God and Father of our Lord Jesus Christ! He is the Father who gives tender love. All comfort comes from him.

—2 CORINTHIANS 1:3–4 NIRV

I will be a Father to you, and you will be my sons and daughters, says the Lord Almighty.

—2 CORINTHIANS 6:18

You have forgotten that word of hope. It speaks to you as children. It says, "My son, think of the Lord's training as important. Do not lose hope when he corrects you. The Lord trains those he loves. He punishes everyone he accepts as a son."
—HEBREWS 12:5–6 NIRV

How great is the love the Father has lavished on us, that we should be called children of God! And that is what we are!
—1 JOHN 3:1

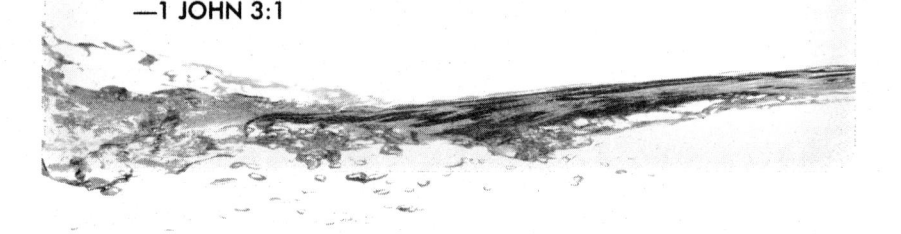

4. Could you talk to a fatherly God like these passages describe? If you are willing, try it.

EPISODE 4

Pure

DISCUSSION

1. How did you find yourself relating to the woman in the story? Did you find yourself liking her, disliking her, connecting with her, criticizing her?

✆ What do you think she was thirsting for in her life?

2. This may be a dangerous question, but in your experience can relationships with other people fulfill the deepest thirsts in our lives?

3. Jesus said He came to:

- proclaim good news to the poor

- announce freedom for prisoners

- bring recovery of sight to the blind

- release the oppressed

§ This claim is recorded in Luke 4. Which needs can you relate to personally?

- Poor: feeling destitute materially, emotionally, relationally, or spiritually

- Captive: boxed in or controlled by others such as your parents, your past, your work situation, or just society in general

- Blind: unable to see clearly, make sense of it all, or figure out how to make life work

- Oppressed: dominated or tormented by inner demons, addictions, anger, or forces that seem to be more powerful than you

4. Which do you sense is most likely to provide you the freedom or power you are looking for to satisfy your deepest needs?

_____ Rules: a solid system of dos and do nots

_____ Stuff: a lot of inanimate material possessions

_____ People: relationships with other human beings

_____ God: a relationship with a divine being

_____ Self: something within, yet untapped

_____ Combination: a mixture of some or all of the above

§ Why do you think so?

5. Kyle claimed that Jesus knows everything about you, yet still loves you. "The one who knows you the best loves you the most."

§ Do you think this is possible? If not, what makes it hard to believe?

6. Kyle tells his story of guacamole. Some of us told our own stories of foods we used to despise but now enjoy.

   § What's the possibility that you have been disliking Jesus, when in reality, if you really knew Him, you would enjoy what He offers?

7. Some religious leaders say, "I will show you the way to truth so you can have real life." Jesus says, "I am the way and the truth and the life" (John 14:6). In another place, He said, "I am the bread of life. He who comes to me will never go hungry, and he who believes in me will never be thirsty" (John 6:35).

   § What do you think of this claim?

8. Complete this sentence: "I believe Jesus (can/cannot/might be able to) quench my thirst because . . ."

～ REFLECTION ～

1. Which of these statements rings true to you?

_____ Jesus can't help me.

_____ Jesus wants nothing to do with me.

_____ Jesus is making an offer too good to be true.

_____ Jesus is more interested in me being good than in me myself.

_____ Jesus is interested in me even though He knows all about me.

2. Try reading the whole story of Jesus and the woman of Samaria as told in John 4. As you do, underline anything that stands out or that you have questions about.

Now he had to go through Samaria. So he came to a town in Samaria called Sychar, near the plot of ground Jacob had given to his son Joseph. Jacob's well was there, and Jesus, tired as he was from the journey, sat down by the well. It was about the sixth hour.

When a Samaritan woman came to draw water, Jesus said to her, "Will you give me a drink?" (His disciples had gone into the town to buy food.) The Samaritan woman said to him, "You are a Jew and I am a Samaritan woman. How can you ask me for a drink?" (For Jews do not associate with Samaritans.)

Jesus answered her, "If you knew the gift of God and who it is that asks you for a drink, you would have asked him and he would have given you living water."

"Sir," the woman said, "you have nothing to draw with and the well is deep. Where can you get this living water? Are you greater than our father Jacob, who gave us the well and drank from it himself, as did also his sons and his flocks and herds?"

Jesus answered, "Everyone who drinks this water will be thirsty again, but whoever drinks the water I give him will never thirst. Indeed, the water I give him will become in him a spring of water welling up to eternal life."

The woman said to him, "Sir, give me this water so that I won't get thirsty and have to keep coming here to draw water."

He told her, "Go, call your husband and come back."

"I have no husband," she replied.

Jesus said to her, "You are right when you say you have no husband. The fact is, you have had five husbands, and the man you now have is not your husband. What you have just said is quite true."

"Sir," the woman said, "I can see that you are a prophet. Our fathers worshiped on this mountain, but you Jews claim that the place where we must worship is in Jerusalem."

Jesus declared, "Believe me, woman, a time is coming when you will worship the Father neither on this mountain nor in Jerusalem. You Samaritans worship what you do not know; we worship what we do know, for salvation is from the Jews. Yet a time is coming and has now come when the true worshipers will worship the Father in spirit and truth, for they are the kind of worshipers the Father seeks. God is spirit, and his worshipers must worship in spirit and in truth."

The woman said, "I know that Messiah (called Christ) is coming." "When he comes, he will explain everything to us."

Then Jesus declared, "I who speak to you am he."

Just then his disciples returned and were surprised to find him talking with a woman. But no one asked, "What do you want?" or "Why are you talking with her?"

Then, leaving her water jar, the woman went back to the town and said to the people, "Come, see a man who told me everything I ever did. Could this be the Christ?" They came out of the town and made their way toward him. . . .

Many of the Samaritans from that town believed in him because of the woman's testimony, "He told me everything I ever did." So when the Samaritans came to him, they urged him to stay with them, and he stayed two days. And because of his words many more became believers.

They said to the woman, "We no longer believe just because of what you said; now we have heard for ourselves, and we know that this man really is the Savior of the world."
—JOHN 4:4–30, 39–42

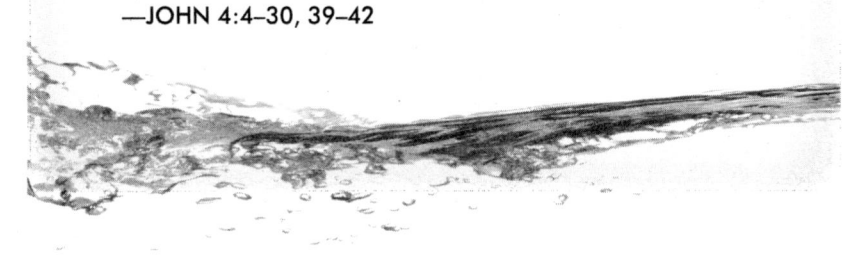

3. Based on what you just read, would Jesus be the kind of person you would like to know?

____ Yes! ____ No! ____ Maybe

✎ Why or why not?

If you would like to know more about Jesus, try reading one of the accounts of His life found in the Bible books of Matthew, Mark, Luke, or John. Start with any of them; they are all good! Use a modern translation that's understandable. If you have a Bible that is difficult to understand, buy a more up-to-date version. Your H2O leader can probably help you choose a good translation. Oftentimes, writing out our thoughts helps us clarify our thinking.

4. Now that you have had four weeks of study, what thoughts or questions do you have about Jesus?

I am the way and the truth and the life.
—JESUS, JOHN 14:6

NOTES

EPISODE 5

Mirage

DISCUSSION

1. Have you ever believed that a certain thing—a car, job, or person—would fulfill you if only you could get it? If you did get it, what was it like? Was it everything you imagined it would be?

2. Do you believe that if, like Solomon, you had just about everything you wanted that you, too, would end up saying, "Meaningless! Meaningless!" (Ecclesiastes 1:2)? Why or why not?

3. In your experience, what can possessions do for you, and what can't they do for you?

4. In your experience, what can achievement give you and what can't it give you?

5. How about relationships? What have you found that they can do for you and what can't they do for you?

6. The purposes Jesus offers us are to know God and live with Him forever as well as to participate in the mission of helping others know God and live with Him forever. How would you compare those purposes with the usual purposes people pursue in life, such as getting rich, raising happy kids, building a big company, or even finding a cure for cancer?

7. How about the security Jesus offers? He says He can guarantee that those who come to Him will never perish, that He can grant them eternal life. Do you think there is life after death, and if so, what do you think it is like? What do you think of Jesus' offer to give ongoing life?

8. It was also claimed that Jesus offers unconditional love, that is, He loves everyone regardless of what they are like. How does this compare to the kind of love you have experienced in the world?

～ REFLECTION ～

1. "If I only had . . . , then I'd be happy!" How would you complete that sentence? If you only had a mate? If you only had a boatload of money? If you could only find the right career? Or maybe it's something as simple as "If I could only get the house cleaned up, the checkbook straightened out, and the kids to school on time!" How would you finish the sentence?

"If I only had _____ , then I'd be happy!"

"If I only had _____ , then I'd be happy!"

"If I only had _____ , then I'd be happy!"

"If I only had _____ , then I'd be happy!"

"If I only had _____ , then I'd be happy!"

2. Is what you are pursuing in an effort to make yourself happy poisoning your life in some way? For example, you might be pursuing corporate success, but it is leading to ulcers and a shaky marriage. Or you might be going from one sexual relationship to another, but this is causing emptiness and regret. Identify any damaging effects to which your efforts to quench your thirst are leading.

3. Consider the following Scripture.

My people have done two evils:
They have turned away from me,
the spring of living water.
And they have dug their own wells,
which are broken wells that cannot hold water.
    —JEREMIAH 2:13 NCV

§ Are our wells really broken?

§ Alfred Adler (psychologist and author) said that everyone needs purpose. What if a person had it all—lots of possessions, great achievements, good looks, and meaningful relationships? Is that enough to provide all the purpose someone would need in life?

§ What about the security Carl Jung (psychologist and anthropologist) said we all need? If we had it all, would that supply all the security we would want?

§ Sigmund Freud (originator of psychoanalysis) said we need love. Would having it all deliver all the love that a human being could ever need?

4. Jesus claims to offer living water, pure water. Based on what you know at this point, how would you describe what He is offering?

____ radiator fluid: it's actually poison, the opiate of the people

____ placebo water: it makes people think they are getting better but it's just a mirage

____ tonic water: it helps; it is good but not necessarily better than other drinks

____ living water: it's the only "good stuff" that can satisfy the deepest thirst

5. Here are some Scriptures that are referred to in the DVD presentation. Circle anything that stands out to you.

The words of the Teacher, son of David, king in Jerusalem:

"Meaningless! Meaningless!"
   says the Teacher.
"Utterly meaningless!
   Everything is meaningless."
What does man gain from all his labor
   at which he toils under the sun? . . .
All things are wearisome,
   more than one can say.
The eye never has enough of seeing,
   nor the ear its fill of hearing.
—ECCLESIASTES 1:1–3, 8

I thought in my heart, "Come now, I will test you with pleasure to find out what is good." But that also proved to be meaningless. "Laughter," I said, "is foolish. And what does pleasure accomplish?" I tried cheering myself with wine, and embracing folly—my mind still guiding me with wisdom. I wanted to see what was worthwhile for men to do under heaven during the few days of their lives.

I undertook great projects: I built houses for myself and planted vineyards. I made gardens and parks and planted all kinds of fruit trees in them. I made reservoirs to water groves of flourishing trees. I bought male and female slaves and had other slaves who were born in my house. I also owned more herds and flocks than anyone in Jerusalem before me. I amassed silver and gold for myself, and the treasure of kings and provinces. I acquired men and women singers, and a harem as well—the delights of the heart of man. I became greater by far than anyone in Jerusalem before me. In all this my wisdom stayed with me.

I denied myself nothing my eyes desired; I refused my heart no pleasure.

My heart took delight in all my work, and this was the reward for all my labor.

Yet when I surveyed all that my hands had done and what I had toiled to achieve, everything was meaningless, a chasing after the wind; nothing was gained under the sun.

—ECCLESIASTES 2:1–11

Can anything ever separate us from Christ's love? Does it mean he no longer loves us if we have trouble or calamity, or are persecuted, or are hungry or cold or in danger or threatened with death? (Even the Scriptures say, "For your sake we are killed every day; we are being slaughtered like sheep.") No, despite all these things, overwhelming victory is ours through Christ, who loved us. And I am convinced that nothing can ever separate us from his love.

Death can't, and life can't. The angels can't, and the demons can't. Our fears for today, our worries about tomorrow, and even the powers of hell can't keep God's love away. Whether we are high above the sky or in the deepest ocean, nothing in all creation will ever be able to separate us from the love of God that is revealed in Christ Jesus our Lord.

—ROMANS 8:35–39 NLT

The Spirit and the bride say, "Come!" And let him who hears say, "Come!" Whoever is thirsty, let him come; and whoever wishes, let him take the free gift of the water of life.

—REVELATION 22:17

6. You may have tried talking to God before. Would you be willing to try writing your thoughts to Him? In a sense, it's just like writing a letter. Write what comes to mind. You may find it therapeutic.

God,
Here are some of my thoughts . . .

NOTES

EPISODE 6

Drowning

~ DISCUSSION ~

1. What are your feelings after watching this segment?

2. Has anyone ever paid your tab or saved you from a mess you couldn't get yourself out of? If so, what was that like for you? How did you find yourself responding to their efforts?

3. What do you think the chances are that God would do something like that for people on earth?

4. Kyle brought up the dreadful Bible word: sin. Do you believe there is such a thing as sin, that is, real wrongdoing?

5. Kyle mentioned four ways people deal with their ugly stuff, their sin.

   • One is to deny it, to just not face it.

   • Another is to rationalize it away. They say things like, "I have a right to be happy; I'm not hurting anybody; I couldn't help it." Someone said that when we rationalize, we are actually telling ourselves "rational lies."

   • Another is to compare themselves with those who are worse— "At least I'm not as bad as so-and-so!"

   • The last is that people try to hide their bad habits—they stash their drug paraphernalia or never tell anyone the hateful thoughts in their heads.

§ Do you think Kyle is right? If so, why do people do these things?

6. One of the big questions about Christianity is, Why does God allow a hell? If a person rebelled against God, wouldn't submit to God, what do you think God should do with such a person?

_____ Let him into heaven anyway (but then God would be letting sin into His perfection and immediately polluting it).

_____ Force this person to surrender (but this would violate his free will, robbing him of his right to choose).

_____ Give the person his wish (but this would mean separation from God and all that is good, that is, existence in outer darkness, or hell).

_____ Create a nice place where sinful, unsubmissive people could go and continue to be sinful and unsubmissive but be as happy as they can be in this state (but this would violate God's justice and be unfair to those who had gone all out to do what was right).

_____ Just annihilate him (but then he wouldn't pay for the wrongs he did commit; people could literally "get away with murder").

7. What did you think of the illustration of the two glasses of water? What do you think God should do with the dark stuff in people's cups?

8. Read Luke 23:33.

> When they came to the place called the Skull, there they crucified him, along with the criminals—one on his right, the other on his left.

§ What stands out to you from this reading?

9. This verse tells what happened to Jesus. But why did it happen? Look at Mark 10:45 (NIRV):

> *Even the Son of Man did not come to be served. Instead, he came to serve others. He came to give his life as the price for setting many people free.*

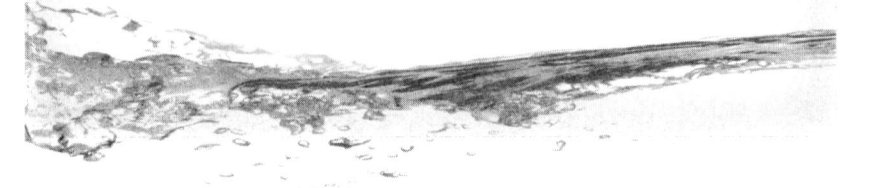

§ Jesus is speaking in this verse. When He uses the title "Son of Man," He is referring to Himself. So what stands out to you from this verse?

10. In the book of Isaiah, we find a prophecy, a sort of advance notification from God about what He was going to do in the future. This was written about seven hundred years before Jesus' time. But it describes what Jesus would do.

> *He suffered the things we should have suffered.*
> *He took on himself the pain that should have been ours.*
> *But we thought God was punishing him.*
> *We thought God was wounding him and making him suffer.*
> *But the servant was pierced because we had sinned.*
> *He was crushed because we had done what was evil.*
> *He was punished to make us whole again.*
> *His wounds have healed us.*
> *All of us are like sheep.*
> *We have wandered away from God.*
> *All of us have turned to our own way.*
> *And the Lord has placed on his servant the sins of all of us.*
> **—ISAIAH 53:4–6 NIRV**

What do you think of this idea of Jesus giving His life to pay the tab for our messing up?

~ REFLECTION ~

1. What we suggest here may be difficult. But to get an honest assessment of your situation, you might decide to try it despite the difficulty.

   To make the most of this time, have a glass half filled with clean water, and a cup of black coffee, cola, or some other dark drink.

   Make a list of the bad stuff you've done. Think about different stages of your life—childhood, high school, college, your young adult years, and so on. Write down whatever unkind, selfish, or harmful things that strike you. It may be as "small" as teasing the neighborhood nerd or stealing pocket change from your mom's purse. It may be as "big" as getting your girlfriend pregnant or screaming profanities at your kids. Take your time. Don't rush. You won't have to show this page to anyone. So whatever comes to mind, write it down.

2. James 4:17 says, "Well, remember that if a man knows what is right and fails to do it, his failure is a real sin" (PHILLIPS).

   If this is true, then what "failure-sins" would you have to add to your list? What should you have done in each stage of life, but didn't? Helped your mom more? Been nice to the neighborhood nerd? Volunteered your time for some worthy cause? Spent time building up your kids? Again, take your time. Mull over things you knew you should have done but neglected.

♪ How do you feel about your list? What is your reaction?

3. If a person did something wrong just five times a day—tell a white lie, gossip about a coworker, blow up at the kids, ignore the nudge to do something good, like call Mom or encourage a friend—in fifty years this person would have accumulated more than ninety thousand offenses!

§ Would you guess your average number of shortcomings per day to be less than or more than five?

___ less than five ___ more than five ___ way more than five!

4. Take your glass of clean water. Add to it the amount of coffee or cola that you think represents how much bad stuff you have done in your life. Try to be honest. (If you're not honest then you have to add "dishonesty" to your list too!)

§ So, how dark is your cup?

§ What will you do with the dark stuff inside?

5. Look back over the Scriptures that were read during the discussion (Luke 23:33; Mark 10:45; Isaiah 53:4–6). What are these passages saying to you now?

Keep your glass and its contents as a visual reminder until our next session. If you are willing, bring it with you to the next gathering.

DISCUSSION

1. What are your thoughts and feelings after watching this episode?
   What questions do you have?

2. Which is closest to how you have responded to God's free offer of a pardon and new life?

- I don't believe it.

- I don't need it.

- I'll try to earn it.

- I don't understand it.

- I don't want it.

- I'll simply accept it.

♪ Put your response to what Jesus is offering in your own words.

3. How are you responding to this offer of a new life?

4. In Kyle's prayer, he mentioned several ways to express new faith in Jesus.

   a. Reject your old way of thinking and acting that was outside God's will. You see your old ways as wrong and decide to do things God's way as best you can. Nobody can do this perfectly, but you decide to try. The Bible calls this *repentance* (Acts 3:19; 17:30; 26:20).

   b. *Confession* is simply saying aloud that you believe Jesus is Lord (Matthew 10:32; Romans 10:9–10; 1 Timothy 6:12–14). In a sense, confession is what you just did when you told this group that you decided to trust Jesus.

   c. *Baptism* is when a person is dipped under water. It is a picture of dying to your old self, of burying your past, being totally cleansed of all your guilt, and being raised up to a new kind of life (Romans 6:3–4; Galatians 3:26–27; 1 Peter 3:20–22). Back when Jesus' first followers were around and the New Testament was being written, a person was always baptized soon after he or she decided to trust Jesus (Acts 2:40–41; 8:26–40; 16:16–30).

   ✆ Does it make sense how these steps can help a person latch on to, or unwrap, God's free gift of salvation?

5. Look at the words to the song "Amazing Grace" printed below. As you listen to and read the lyrics, if you feel moved to do so, please feel free to exchange your dirty glass of water for a fresh one under the cross.

Amazing grace! How sweet the sound
That saved a wretch like me!
I once was lost, but now I'm found;
Was blind, but now I see.

'Twas grace that taught my heart to fear,
And grace my fear relieved;
How precious did that grace appear
The hour I first believed!

Through many dangers, toils and snares,
I have already come;
'Tis grace hath brought me safe thus far,
And grace will lead me home.

When we've been there ten thousand years,
Bright shining as the sun,
We've no less days to sing God's praise
Than when we'd first begun.
 —JOHN NEWTON, 1779

6. For those of you who exchanged your glasses at the cross, how did that feel? What was your reaction?

REFLECTION

1. Do you have a sense that you have met God or interacted with Him in some way during your H2O experience? If so, what was that like? What did you make of it?

2. Where do you see yourself going next in your spiritual journey?

3. If you are not ready to accept Jesus' free offer of forgiveness of sins and escape from the death penalty, what's the reason?

_____ I don't think the offer is real.

_____ I don't need the help; I'm not that bad.

_____ I refuse to accept anyone's charity; I should pay for my own mistakes.

_____ I just feel too guilty to believe that I can ever be released from my guilt.

_____ I know I can't live up to it; I'll end up going back to my old ways.

_____ Other: _____

4. The following passages of Scripture have been paraphrased for this exercise. They describe what Jesus has done for us and what it means for us. Personalize them by writing your name in each of the blanks.

When they came to the place called the Skull, there they crucified him, along with the criminals—one on his right, the other on his left.

Jesus said, "Father, forgive _____ , for _____ does not know what he or she is doing."
   —LUKE 23:33–34

For God so loved _____ that he gave his one and only Son, that if _____ believes in him _____ shall not perish but have eternal life.
   —JOHN 3:16

God saved _____ by his special favor when _____ believed.

And _____ can't take credit for this; it is a gift from God.

Salvation is not a reward for the good things _____ has done, so none of us including _____ can boast about it.

For _____ is God's masterpiece.

He has created _____ anew in Christ Jesus, so that _____ can do the good things he planned for _____ long ago.
   —EPHESIANS 2:8–10 NLT

Christ never sinned but God put _____'s sin on Him.

Then _____ is made right with God because of what Christ has done for _____ .

—2 CORINTHIANS 5:21 NLV

5. Try reading these passages aloud with your name in them. What is that like?

If you would like to find out what happened after Jesus' death, read Luke 24.

NOTES

EPISODE 8

Clean

DISCUSSION

1. What's your reaction to the idea that the Christian life is living out new, God-given identities rather than following a list of rules?

2. What's the difference between someone trying to follow the rules and someone living out of a new nature?

3. Kyle discussed three identities that the heavenly Father gives to those who turn to Him. The first is a *child*. Read 1 John 3:1.

How great is the love the Father has lavished on us, that we should be called children of God! And that is what we are!

♪ If a person really believes he or she is a child of God, and accepts that as a core identity, what effect might it have on his or her life?

4. A second identity is a *sojourner* or *traveler* in this world. One of Jesus' closest followers, Peter, wrote to his fellow believers:

> *Dear friends, I urge you, as aliens and strangers in the world, to . . .*
> **—1 PETER 2:11**

♪ How would you finish that sentence?

♪ Here is how Peter finished his own sentence:

> *Dear friends, I urge you, as aliens and strangers in the world, to abstain from sinful desires, which war against your soul.*

§ How does the way Peter finished his sentence line up with the way your group finished it?

5. A third identity is an *athlete*. Look at 1 Corinthians 9:25:

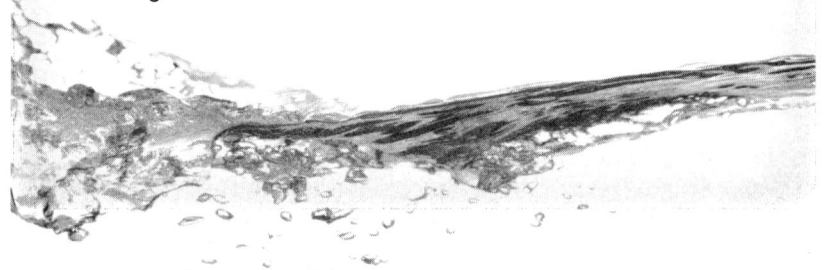

> *Everyone who competes in the games goes into strict training. They do it to get a crown that will not last; but we do it to get a crown that will last forever.*

§ Do you run or work out? What's your regimen?

♪ If you were to tell someone how to get started, what would you advise?

♪ Would you advise training versus simply trying?

6. Of the three images—child, traveler, and athlete—which do you connect with right away? Which do you find hardest to relate to?

7. If you saw yourself as these three things—child, traveler, athlete—what would change in your life? Would that be a good change, a bad change, a scary change? How would you characterize it?

~ REFLECTION ~

1. For each identity that you listed in the Discussion section, write beside it what that identity leads you to do or be. For example, if you listed "teacher," that might lead you to find students, prepare lessons, or keep on learning.

2. Are there any of these identities that you would like to be rid of? If so, which ones, and why?

3. How does someone receive these new identities that God gives? John 1:12–13 (NCV) describes how someone becomes a child of God, the first identity Kyle talked about.

But to all who did accept him [Jesus] and believe in him he gave the right to become children of God. They did not become his children in any human way—by any human parents or human desire. They were born of God.

§ According to this passage, how does this happen?

4. What's your last name? _____

   § How did you get this last name?

5. What, if anything, goes along with having this last name? For instance, maybe you are a Jones, and the Joneses always play a lot of sports, graduate from college, and make good in the business world. Or you are a Smith, and the Smiths love music, eat pasta, and laugh a lot. What goes along with your last name?

6. Have you lived out this family identity, pushed away from it, or maybe done a bit of both?

7. Those who decide to trust what God has done through Jesus are automatically given the Father's name and become His children. It is not something we must *earn*, but it is something we must *learn*. We learn how to be the child of God we have become.

§ What might it be like to live out of this family identity?

§ Will you accept this family identity?

EPISODE 9

Vapor

DISCUSSION

1. What are your reactions to this week's episode?

2. One of the roles of the Holy Spirit is to comfort believers in times of trouble. Have you had such an experience of God's comfort?

3. How about God's Spirit teaching believers and acting as our moral compass—a kind of global positioning system? Have you ever experienced that?

4. How can you know the difference between your own intuition and a nudge from the Spirit or between the voice of conscience and the leading of the Holy Spirit?

5. Another aspect of the Holy Spirit's work is that He communicates for us in prayer. How does this truth give the believer assurance that his or her prayers are heard and understood by God the Father?

6. One big question to consider is, How does someone receive this Spirit and really utilize His power? The book of Acts looks at Jesus' promise to His twelve special disciples called apostles.

§ Acts is in the New Testament, the last third of the Bible. Acts comes right after Matthew, Mark, Luke, and John. Those books tell the story of Jesus. Then Acts tells the story of the early believers in Jesus.

§ The events in Acts take place after Jesus died on the cross. His apostles thought it was all over, but three days later they met Jesus alive. God had raised Him from the dead to confirm that Jesus was innocent and that He really was the Son of God. Now Jesus is about to leave them and return to heaven. Read 1:4–9.

On one occasion, while he was eating with them, he gave them this command: "Do not leave Jerusalem, but wait for the gift my Father promised, which you have heard me speak about. For John baptized with water, but in a few days you will be baptized with the Holy Spirit."

So when they met together, they asked him, "Lord, are you at this time going to restore the kingdom to Israel?"

He said to them: "It is not for you to know the times or dates the Father has set by his own authority. But you will receive power when the Holy Spirit comes on you; and you will be my witnesses in Jerusalem, and in all Judea and Samaria, and to the ends of the earth."

After he said this, he was taken up before their very eyes, and a cloud hid him from their sight.

ⓢ Jesus promised the apostles they would receive power when the Spirit came. Acts 2 recounts the first time the Holy Spirit came upon/filled the apostles. Because of this special gift, the apostles were able to preach in all the languages of the Jews who had gathered in Jerusalem for a holiday called Pentecost. When the crowd was confused about what they were witnessing, Peter stood and addressed them all. He told them what Jesus did for everyone—how He died and then rose from the dead. Look at verse 37:

When the people heard this, they were cut to the heart and said to Peter and the other apostles, "Brothers, what shall we do?"

ⓢ Peter's reply is important. Verse 38 explains how someone receives the Spirit.

Repent and be baptized, every one of you, in the name of Jesus Christ for the forgiveness of your sins. And you will receive the gift of the Holy Spirit.

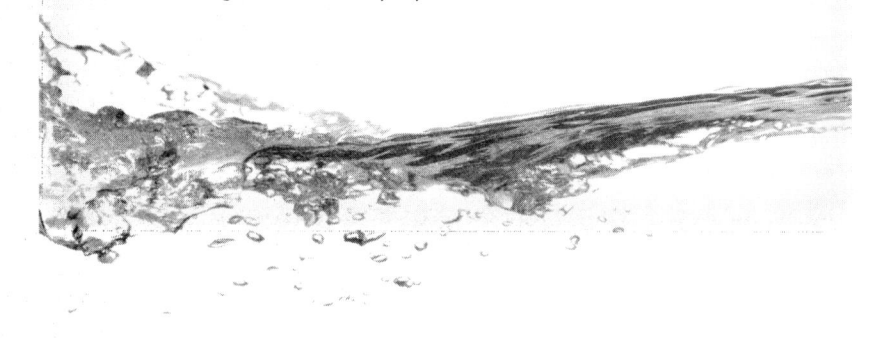

§ So, who has the Spirit living in them?

7. If every believer in Jesus has the Spirit, then why don't they always feel His power, guidance, and comfort?

REFLECTION

1. What questions do you still have about the Holy Spirit?

2. Would you like to have the gift of the Holy Spirit? Why or why not?

3. Read the following verses from Luke and Ephesians.

> *Would any of you who are fathers give your son a snake when he asks for fish? Or would you give him a scorpion when he asks for an egg? As bad as you are, you know how to give good things to your children. How much more, then, will the Father in heaven give the Holy Spirit to those who ask him!*
>
> **—LUKE 11:11–13 GNT**

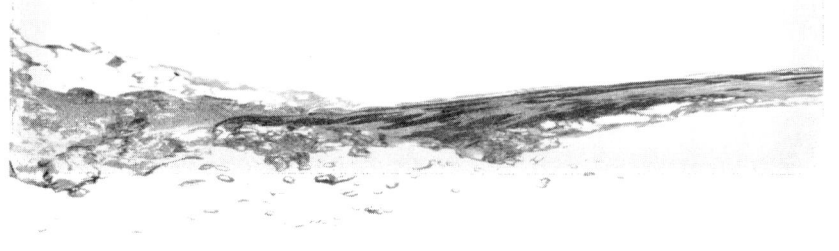

> *Therefore do not be foolish, but understand what the Lord's will is. Do not get drunk on wine, which leads to debauchery. Instead, be filled with the Spirit.*
> —EPHESIANS 5:17–18

֍ What do you conclude about God's desire for us to have the Holy Spirit?

4. What difference do you think the gift of the Spirit could make in your life?

5. How will you respond to the promise and the command Jesus makes in the passages on pages 105 and 106?

6. The DVD encouraged us to fill ourselves with the Word of God in order to be filled with the Spirit. To connect with the Spirit, it helps to have some knowledge of the Spirit. Take time this week to meditate on these Bible passages about the Spirit. Underline or circle ideas you want to remember, ask about, or test in your own life.

"God's Spirit gives new life."

Jesus replied, "I tell you for certain that you must be born from above before you can see God's kingdom!" Nicodemus asked, "How can a grown man ever be born a second time?" Jesus answered: I tell you for certain that before you can get into God's kingdom, you must be born not only by water, but by the Spirit. Humans give life to their children. Yet only God's Spirit can change you into a child of God. Don't be surprised when I say that you must be born from above. Only God's Spirit gives new life. The Spirit is like the wind that blows wherever it wants to. You can hear the wind, but you don't know where it comes from or where it is going.
—JOHN 3:3–8 CEV

The Holy Spirit causes "rivers of living water" to flow in the lives of believers.

On the last day, the climax of the holidays, Jesus shouted to the crowds, "If anyone is thirsty, let him come to me and drink. For the Scriptures declare that rivers of living water shall flow from the inmost being of anyone who believes in me." (He was speaking of the Holy Spirit, who would be given to everyone believing in him; but the Spirit had not yet been given, because Jesus had not yet returned to his glory in heaven.)

—JOHN 7:37–39 TLB

The Spirit guides us to the truth.

I still have many things to tell you, but you can't handle them now. But when the Friend comes, the Spirit of the Truth, he will take you by the hand and guide you into all the truth there is. He won't draw attention to himself, but will make sense out of what is about to happen and, indeed, out of all that I have done and said. He will honor me; he will take from me and deliver it to you.

—JOHN 16:12–14 MSG

The Holy Spirit is a Counselor who lives within believers.

And I will ask the Father, and he will give you another Counselor to be with you forever—the Spirit of truth. The world cannot accept him, because it neither sees him nor knows him. But you know him, for he lives with you and will be in you. I will not leave you as orphans; I will come to you.

—JOHN 14:16–18

The Holy Spirit reminds Christians of Jesus' teachings.

I am telling you these things now while I am still with you. But when the Father sends the Counselor as my representative—and by the Counselor I mean the Holy Spirit—he will teach you everything and will remind you of everything I myself have told you. I am leaving you with a gift—peace of mind and heart. And the peace I give isn't like the peace the world gives. So don't be troubled or afraid.
    —JOHN 14:25–27 NLT

Those who repent and are baptized "receive the gift of the Holy Spirit."

When the people heard this [the truth about Jesus], they were cut to the heart and said to Peter and the other apostles, "Brothers, what shall we do?" Peter replied, "Repent and be baptized, every one of you, in the name of Jesus Christ for the forgiveness of your sins. And you will receive the gift of the Holy Spirit. The promise is for you and your children and for all who are far off—for all whom the Lord our God will call."
    —ACTS 2:37–39

The Spirit reminds us "that we are God's children."

The Spirit himself testifies with our spirit that we are God's children.
    —ROMANS 8:16

The Holy Spirit prays for us when we don't know how to pray.

And the Holy Spirit helps us in our distress. For we don't even know what we should pray for, nor how we should pray. But the Holy Spirit prays for us with groanings that cannot be expressed in words. And the Father who knows all hearts knows what the Spirit is saying, for the Spirit pleads for us believers in harmony with God's own will.

—ROMANS 8:26–27 NLT

One day we will be raised to eternal life by God's Spirit.

You are no longer ruled by your desires, but by God's Spirit, who lives in you. People who don't have the Spirit of Christ in them don't belong to him. But Christ lives in you. So you are alive because God has accepted you, even though your bodies must die because of your sins. Yet God raised Jesus to life! God's Spirit now lives in you, and he will raise you to life by his Spirit.

—ROMANS 8:9–11 CEV

God's Spirit helps us to have those qualities that make us more like Jesus.

God's Spirit makes us loving, happy, peaceful, patient, kind, good, faithful, gentle, and self-controlled. There is no law against behaving in any of these ways. And because we belong to Christ Jesus, we have killed our selfish feelings and desires. God's Spirit has given us life, and so we should follow the Spirit.

—GALATIANS 5:22–25 CEV

You'll be having an H2O party soon, so be thinking about whom you might like to invite to come with you. Or even better, ask the Spirit to bring to mind those you might ask and then give you the courage to ask them.

EPISODE 10

The River

~ DISCUSSION ~

1. If you knew of a place to belong like Kyle described, would you be part of it? Why or why not?

§ Do you think it is possible that there are groups of people like that?

2. What's the best group you've ever been a part of—a ball team, a club, maybe your own family?

৪ What made it so good?

৪ Was there anything bad about it? Any shortcomings?

3. No matter how good a group might be, there will also be some negatives. But in worthwhile groups, the good outweighs the bad. The DVD portrayed several nightmare versions of church.

§ What would be your biggest fear of going to church?

§ Would it be worth facing this fear if you could find a place like Kyle described?

4. One aspect of a healthy church is *no irrelevant teaching*. Read Acts 2:42–47.

> *They devoted themselves to the apostles' teaching and to the fellowship, to the breaking of bread and to prayer. Everyone was filled with awe, and many wonders and miraculous signs were done by the apostles. All the believers were together and had everything in common. Selling their possessions and goods, they gave to anyone as he had need. Every day they continued to meet together in the temple courts. They broke bread in their homes and ate together with glad and sincere hearts, praising God and enjoying the favor of all the people. And the Lord added to their number daily those who were being saved.*

§ What makes teaching relevant, worthwhile, and meaningful?

§ Why would anyone go to a church where the teaching isn't relevant?

§ How would listening to uninteresting, unintelligible, or meaningless teaching week after week affect someone?

5. Another aspect of a healthy church is that no one stands alone. Why do people try to stand alone in life?

§ What happens to them when they do?

§ How do you connect with others?

6. Another rule Kyle gave was that the church should be a place where *masks aren't worn*. Kyle noted the word *sincere* in verse 46. The early Christians were real.

§ What leads people to wear masks?

§ Would you really want to be a part of a group where the masks came off?

§ How could a person have enough courage to take off their mask?

♪ What if a person really accepted the truth that he is a child of God—could he take off the mask then?

7. The fifth rule was *no perfect people allowed, only changed people.* These people in Acts were doing a lot of good things—selling their possessions, helping the poor, praising God. But notice the last line of verse 47: "The Lord added to their number daily those who were being saved." It doesn't say they were perfect but that they were saved, being changed into what God really wanted. The church should be a place where people are growing and getting better.

♪ How have you been changed during this series?

8. What's next for you on your spiritual journey?

 REFLECTION

1. What is your overall response to H2O and its message?

2. What would you say you learned?

3. What did you decide during this course?

4. What questions do you still have?

5. Whom would you like to invite to the next H2O?

6. How about writing a prayer to God in response to this course? Say whatever you sincerely think or feel. Maybe add a prayer that those you invite to the next session of H2O would be open to trying it.

These Scriptures were mentioned in Episode 10.

They devoted themselves to the apostles' teaching and to the fellowship, to the breaking of bread and to prayer. Everyone was filled with awe, and many wonders and miraculous signs were done by the apostles. All the believers were together and had everything in common. Selling their possessions and goods, they gave to anyone as he had need. Every day they continued to meet together in the temple courts. They broke bread in their homes and ate together with glad and sincere hearts, praising God and enjoying the favor of all the people. And the Lord added to their number daily those who were being saved.
   —**ACTS 2:42–47**

When Jesus had finished saying these things, the crowds were amazed at his teaching, because he taught as one who had authority, and not as their teachers of the law.
   —**MATTHEW 7:28–29**

For the word of God is living and active. Sharper than any double-edged sword, it penetrates even to dividing soul and spirit, joints and marrow; it judges the thoughts and attitudes of the heart.
   —**HEBREWS 4:12**

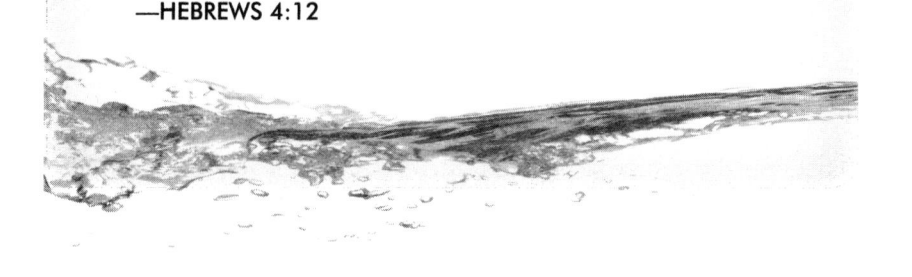

You, my brothers, were called to be free. But do not use your freedom to indulge the sinful nature; rather, serve one another in love. The entire law is summed up in a single command: "Love your neighbor as yourself."
—GALATIANS 5:13–14

Therefore encourage one another and build each other up, just as in fact you are doing.
—1 THESSALONIANS 5:11

Accept one another, then, just as Christ accepted you, in order to bring praise to God.
—ROMANS 15:7

Then I saw a new heaven and a new earth, for the first heaven and the first earth had passed away, and there was no longer any sea. I saw the Holy City, the new Jerusalem, coming down out of heaven from God, prepared as a bride beautifully dressed for her husband. And I heard a loud voice from the throne saying, "Now the dwelling of God is with men, and he will live with them. They will be his people, and God himself will be with them and be their God. He will wipe every tear from their eyes. There will be no more death or mourning or crying or pain, for the old order of things has passed away."
—REVELATION 21:1–4

Then the angel showed me the river of the water of life, as clear as crystal, flowing from the throne of God and of the Lamb down the middle of the great street of the city. On each side of the river stood the tree of life, bearing twelve crops of fruit, yielding its fruit every month. And the leaves of the tree are for the healing of the nations. No longer will there be any curse. The throne of God and of the Lamb will be in the city, and his servants will serve him.

They will see his face, and his name will be on their foreheads. There will be no more night. They will not need the light of a lamp or the light of the sun, for the Lord God will give them light. And they will reign for ever and ever.

—REVELATION 22:1–5